D0583529

MILITARY SPECIAL OPS

ARMY RANGERS

ELITE OPERATIONS

BY MARCIA AMIDON LUSTED

Lerner Publications Company
A division of Lerner Publishing Group, Inc.
241 First Avenue North
Minneapolis, MN 55401 U.S.A.

Website address: www.lernerbooks.com

Content Consultant: Kalev Sepp, assistant professor, Naval Postgraduate School

Library of Congress Cataloging-in-Publication Data
Lusted, Marcia Amidon.
    Army Rangers : elite operations / Marcia Amidon Lusted.
        pages   cm. — (Military special ops)
    Includes index.
    ISBN 978–0–7613–9078–7 (lib. bdg. : alk. paper)
    ISBN 978–1–4677–1763–2 (eBook)
    1. United States. Army. Ranger Regiment, 75th—Juvenile literature.
    2. United States. Army—Commando troops—Juvenile literature. I. Title.
UA34.R36L87   2014
356'.1670973—dc23   2013001737

Manufactured in the United States of America
1 — MG — 7/15/13

The images in this book are used with the permission of: Pedro Amador/ U.S. Army, 5; Brian Kohl/U.S. Army, 6; Manuel Menedez/U.S. Army, 7; Clay Lancaster/U.S. Army, 8; © AP Images, 11, 12; Julianne Showalter/ U.S. Air Force, 13, 22; Tony Hawkins/U.S. Army, 15; © Dave Ekren/ AP Images, 16; Marcus Butler/United States Army Special Operations Command, 17; U.S. Army, 18, 26; Adam Hesley/U.S. Army, 19; Samuel Goodman/U.S. Army, 21; Teddy Wade/U.S. Army, 23; Giancarlo Casem/U.S. Army, 25; John D. Helms/U.S. Army, 27; Daren Reehl/United States Army Special Operations Command, 28.

Front cover: © Stocktrek Images/SuperStock.

Main body text set in Tw Cen MT Std Medium 12/18.
Typeface provided by Adobe Systems.

CONTENTS

CHAPTER ONE:
ATTACK ON BAGRAM

It was 3:30 A.M., May 19, 2010, at Bagram Airfield in Afghanistan. Out of the darkness, explosions lit up the sky. Afghan soldiers who were loyal to the Taliban were attacking the airfield's two main entrances. They shot rockets and damaged a building on the base. They attacked U.S. guards with handguns and grenades. Some of the attackers were suicide bombers. They wore vests packed with explosives.

SUICIDE BOMBERS

One of the most lethal weapons used by terrorists is actually a person. It is the suicide bomber. Suicide bombers are willing to kill themselves so they can kill many others at the same time. They wear a vest stuffed with explosives. The terrorist might also pack nails and broken glass, called shrapnel, around the explosives. When the vest explodes, the shrapnel flies through the air and wounds anyone it reaches. Suicide bombers hide the vest under their clothes. They keep a small detonator in a pocket. They sneak into a crowded area or a military base. Then they set off the explosives. The terrorist bomber dies. Many people around him or her are killed or injured as well.

Army Rangers in Afghanistan wait for pickup by helicopter.

The current conflict in Afghanistan began after the terrorist attacks against the United States on September 11, 2001. The terrorists had strongholds in Afghanistan. The United States sent military forces there to wipe them out. Bagram became the U.S. military's most important base in Afghanistan. Among the soldiers inside the base were Rangers from the U.S. Army's 75th Ranger Regiment. They had arrived at Bagram the night before. An explosion rocked the walls of the base. Someone called for a medic. The Rangers quickly scrambled for their weapons.

Ranger Sergeant First Class Michael Eiermann found his unit's medic. With a handful of Rangers, they ran toward the wall. Eiermann discovered two wounded U.S. soldiers. The soldiers had been caught in a minefield outside the airfield. They had been wounded in a land mine explosion. The rebels were shooting at Eiermann and his Rangers. But the Rangers were able to treat the wounded soldiers and move them to safety.

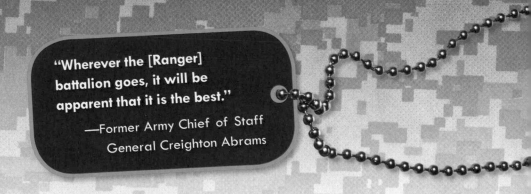

Meanwhile, other Rangers were fighting the rebels, keeping them from breaking into the base. Soon U.S. Army helicopter gunships joined the fight. Several of the rebels were killed, and the rest were driven off. No U.S. soldiers died thanks to the quick actions of the Rangers.

Sergeant Eiermann received the Silver Star for rescuing his fellow soldiers. It is the third-highest award the army gives for bravery. But Eiermann just said, "To me, they were guys who needed help, and my medic and I were in the right place with the right resources to [give] aid, so we did."

Rangers practice carrying a wounded soldier to safety.

Eiermann and the other Rangers at Bagram demonstrated what it means to be an Army Ranger. They had just arrived at the airfield. But they were ready to defend the base and help other soldiers. They used their skills and training to lead a counterattack. The Rangers are the U.S. Army's best special operations unit for making surprise attacks against strongly defended targets. They can attack from the land, sea, or air.

Rangers can get on the ground in a hurry.

RESCUING PRISONERS OF WAR

During World War II (1939–1945), Rangers helped rescue more than five hundred Allied prisoners of war. They were held in a Japanese prison camp at Cabanatuan in the Philippines. A group of 121 Rangers went behind enemy lines. Eighty friendly Filipinos who were fighting the Japanese to free their country helped. The Rangers and the Filipinos watched the camp, observing and planning. When the time was right, they surrounded it. An American P-61 airplane specially made for nighttime raids distracted the Japanese soldiers. This allowed the Rangers and Filipinos to sneak into the camp under the cover of darkness. Their attack lasted only thirty minutes. They got all the prisoners to safety before the Japanese could counterattack.

The Rangers' regimental motto is *Sua sponte*. This is Latin for "Of their own accord." This is because every Army Ranger has volunteered three times. First, he volunteered to enlist in the U.S. Army. Then he volunteered for Airborne School. Finally, he volunteered to join the Rangers. The Army Rangers are dedicated men. They are part of a long tradition. Rangers have served the United States since colonial days. Their unofficial motto is "Rangers lead the way!" They are often the first ones into battle. They go wherever they are ordered to go. They do whatever needs to be done.

CHAPTER TWO: "RANGERS LEAD THE WAY"

The Rangers' history goes back before the earliest days of the United States. The Rangers started in 1756. This was during the French and Indian War (1754–1763), before the American colonies were independent. These early Rangers used the skills frontiersmen used to survive in the wild. Then they fought during the Revolutionary War (1775–1783). They later joined other conflicts, such as the U.S. Civil War (1861–1865). But the Army Rangers did not exist as a unit during peacetime. When another war began, a new group of Rangers would assemble.

ARMY ORGANIZATION

The 75th Ranger Regiment is organized like a pyramid. The full regiment is the tip of the pyramid. Below are the three battalions. Each battalion has three companies (A, B, and C), plus a staff at headquarters. Companies have 152 Rangers each. These are divided into four platoons: three rifle platoons and one weapons platoon. Each company also has a headquarters staff. Platoons are divided into smaller squads of just a few Rangers.

The regiment also includes a Special Troops Battalion. This is made of companies that specialize in reconnaissance, information gathering, communications, and support jobs.

An early Ranger trains for action during World War II.

In 1941 U.S. Army Brigadier General Lucian Truscott was ordered to create a group of "super infantry." They were needed to fight in World War II. These carefully selected soldiers would receive expert training in weapons and combat. They would go on special scouting and patrolling missions. They would launch raids, ambushes, cliff assaults, water attacks, and night operations. Truscott copied the training and organization of the British Commandos. However, he wanted to give his Americans a different name. He remembered the important role of Rangers in earlier American wars. So he named the new unit Rangers.

Rangers practice storming a beach during World War II.

During World War II, the Rangers earned their famous motto. They led assaults on the beaches of Normandy, France, on D-day, June 6, 1944. The Rangers climbed steep cliffs 100 feet (30 meters) high to destroy an enemy gun battery. These guns could have devastated the Allied forces below. The Rangers scaled the cliffs under heavy fire from the enemy. Then the Rangers sent out scouts to find the enemy guns. When they did, they destroyed the guns with explosives. At the same time, down on the beaches, other Rangers landed with infantry divisions. The Germans fired at the Rangers and the infantry with machine guns and mortars. There were many casualties. The other infantrymen hesitated to move up the beach. Then an American general saw the Rangers. He knew they were elite troops. He went to them and shouted, "Rangers, lead the way!" Ultimately, the Allies won the bloody battle. Throughout the war, the Rangers performed many dangerous missions and received many awards.

Rangers served during the Korean War (1950–1953) and the Vietnam War. The 1st and 2nd Ranger Battalions were created in 1974. In 1986 a third battalion was added. The three combined to form the 75th Ranger Regiment. Another three training battalions form a permanent Ranger Training Brigade. The training brigade operates the Ranger School at Fort Benning, Georgia. It does not perform combat missions.

Rangers load a plane for a parachute jump exercise at Fort Benning in Georgia.

CHAPTER THREE: READY AT A MOMENT'S NOTICE

The Rangers have been a permanent part of the army since 1974, even during times of peace. The Rangers are flexible, highly trained, and can move quickly when they are needed. They are an important part of special operations missions. They have served in places such as Iran, Grenada, Afghanistan, and Haiti.

The Rangers are a light infantry unit. But what exactly does this mean? A light infantry unit fights where tanks and armored vehicles cannot go. They fight in mountains, swamps, and forests and inside buildings. As light infantry, the Rangers are ready to go anywhere at a moment's notice. Rangers are often the first ones on the scene of a conflict. They are skilled at dropping into combat zones by parachute or from helicopters. They can survive hidden in the wild for days. They are good at gathering information about the enemy.

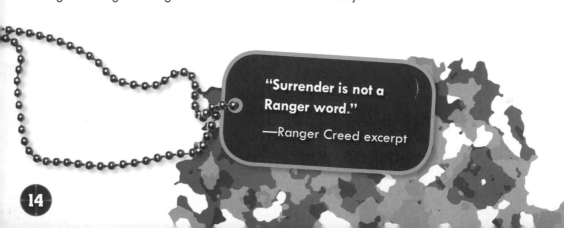

"Surrender is not a Ranger word."

—Ranger Creed excerpt

Rangers must be experts at parachuting.

In 1983 the Rangers showed they were always ready for action. The island of Grenada in the Caribbean was taken over by a rebel group. The U.S. government worried that American university students on the island were in danger. Rangers were ready to go just hours after they learned of the situation. They did not have accurate maps of the island. They didn't know how well defended it was. But Rangers are trained to think on their feet to accomplish difficult tasks.

Rangers return home from their successful Grenada mission.

Rangers specialize in quick surprise strikes.

Rangers parachuted into the airport at Point Salines in Grenada. Then they called in U.S. Air Force gunships to help secure the area. Rangers cleared the runway so other army units could land. Then they rescued students trapped at one of the island's college campuses. They soon found out that more students were being held at another location. The Rangers freed the students and drove back enemy attacks. The Rangers hadn't known what to expect on the island, but they were able to complete their mission.

Rangers can arrive quickly at the scene of a battle or other dangerous situation. They see what's going on and what needs to be done, and they do it. They are especially good at conducting surprise raids on the enemy. They are sometimes called shock troops because they are so good at surprise strikes.

Army Rangers patrol a street at night in Iraq in 2007.

Rangers have seized airfields from enemy control to allow friendly military forces to land. Rangers captured an airfield in Panama in just two hours during a 1989 invasion. During Operation Desert Storm in Iraq in 1991, they secured remote airfields. They also conducted raids and went on scouting missions. They destroyed enemy missiles and helped train troops. At times they were 100 miles (160 kilometers) behind enemy lines and near hostile Iraqi troops. But they were never discovered.

Rangers can deploy anywhere in the world in just eighteen hours. The three Ranger combat battalions take turns being the Ranger Ready Force (RRF). They stand duty for thirteen weeks at a time. During this time, the battalion is not allowed to train away from their home base.

Ranger training prepares soldiers to be ready at a moment's notice.

The soldiers are vaccinated against diseases common in the parts of the world where they might be sent. All weapons are checked, repaired, and replaced if needed. Mission supplies are packed into crates. Everything is ready to ship immediately if called for.

MISSION IN FOCUS   SOMALIA

The Rangers added to their reputation for courage during a mission in Somalia in 1993. Six warlords were fighting for control of the country. They were stealing supplies sent by other countries to help the people of Somalia. One hundred and twenty Rangers supported forty Army Delta Force troops. Together they flew to the Somali city of Mogadishu in helicopters. They fast-roped onto the roof of a building where some of the warlords were meeting. Delta Force troops captured the warlords while the Rangers provided security. The U.S. troops were ambushed and surrounded on the way out of the city. The Rangers and the Delta Force troops fought their way out of the city through more than one thousand enemy gunmen. Eighteen U.S. military members died during the action. Two Delta Force operators who died received the Medal of Honor for heroism. The Medal of Honor is the highest U.S. military honor. Ranger captain Michael Steele received a Bronze Star for his actions.

CHAPTER FOUR:
GEARING UP

Most of the Rangers' weapons and equipment is the U.S. Army's standard issue. But their training prepares them to use whatever is handy to get the job done. In the earliest days of the United States, Rangers fought with hatchets as well as rifles. Rangers fighting in the invasion of Normandy during World War II used the Bangalore Torpedo. This long pipe filled with explosives was invented for clearing minefields. The Rangers also used it to blow holes in fences, walls, and wire. Today Rangers use explosives, electrical tape, plastic ties called flex-cuff, and lengths of metal fencing to get through obstacles.

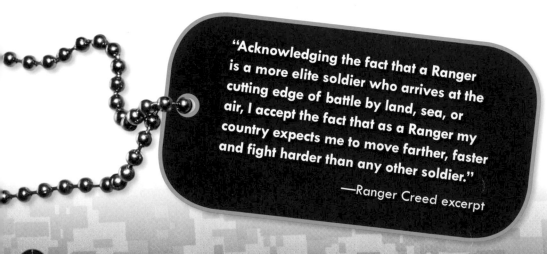

"Acknowledging the fact that a Ranger is a more elite soldier who arrives at the cutting edge of battle by land, sea, or air, I accept the fact that as a Ranger my country expects me to move farther, faster and fight harder than any other soldier."

—Ranger Creed excerpt

A Ranger practices firing a light-weight mortar during a training exercise with live ammunition.

A Ranger's basic weapon is the M4 carbine. Some carry M16 rifles with a M203 40-millimeter grenade launcher. They also use M240 and M249 machine guns. Ranger units have mortars and the Ranger Antitank Weapon System (RAWS). The RAWS looks like a tube with a shoulder mount and two grips. It does not recoil when it is fired. A soldier can use it while standing, sitting, lying down, or kneeling. It can take out lightly armored vehicles and some fortified buildings.

Rangers often make parachute jumps with 60-pound (27-kilogram) packs.

Rangers also carry modern tools of war. They use infrared devices for aiming and night-vision equipment. They carry ammunition, food, water, radios, flares, grenades, and other weapons. All the gear Rangers carry can weigh 100 pounds (45 kg). Rangers must be strong so they can move quickly and even jump out of airplanes with this load.

THE RANGER HANDBOOK

Rangers carry a copy of the Ranger Handbook. This pocket-sized book has everything a Ranger might need to know, from bad weather survival tips to using explosives. A Ranger gets this book during training and keeps it for reference.

Rangers wear the same uniform that regular army soldiers do. This is usually camouflage. They also wear either a cloth cap or a protective combat helmet. Members of the 75th Ranger Regiment sometimes wear a tan beret. Rangers wear a shoulder patch shaped like a scroll. It tells what Ranger battalion they belong to. Soldiers who complete Ranger School wear special tabs on their sleeves. Combat boots complete the uniform.

This member of the 1st Ranger Battalion also wears the tab showing he has completed Ranger School.

CHAPTER FIVE:
RANGER SCHOOL

A Ranger might look like any other army soldier. But his tan beret shows he is part of a very elite group. A Ranger needs to be disciplined, tough, a good leader, smart, and in excellent physical shape.

All Rangers must complete the Ranger Assessment and Selection Program (RASP). Candidates are tested as they learn the skills they need to join the 75th Ranger Regiment. They must prove their physical fitness, marksmanship, and mental toughness. Members of the 75th Ranger Regiment must also finish Airborne School, where they learn to parachute. Ranger officers attend Ranger School, as do Rangers

RASP REQUIREMENTS

Candidates must measure up to the following standards to pass RASP:

- ★ A 5-mile (8 km) run in less than forty minutes
- ★ A 12-mile (19 km) march with a 35-pound (16 kg) pack in less than three hours
- ★ Meet high army standards for sit-ups, push-ups, and chin-ups
- ★ Pass a swimming test

who have served for a while. Soldiers who aren't members of the 75th Ranger Regiment can also attend. Ranger School is one of the most challenging programs in the U.S. Army. At least 65 percent of soldiers who attend Ranger School drop out.

Ranger School lasts sixty-one days, but because it is so difficult, many students first go through a one-month preparation course. This focuses on physical training and basic military skills.

A soldier trains to enter Ranger school. Each phase of Ranger training requires higher levels of physical and mental toughness.

"[Our goal is] to produce a hardened, competent, small-unit leader who is confident he can lead his unit into combat and overcome all obstacles to accomplish his mission."

—Mission of the U.S. Army Ranger School

Then they go to Ranger School. The training is divided between three different army bases. Soldiers train in the forests around Fort Benning, the mountains near Dahlonega, Georgia, and the swamps of the Florida Panhandle.

The first phase is basic Ranger training. This is called the Darby Phase, or Fort Benning Phase. Soldiers learn the physical and military skills they need to complete the rest of Ranger School successfully. Training can last twenty-one hours a day. Students face warlike

Ranger School students practice mission planning during Fort Benning Phase.

situations. They don't get enough sleep or food. They have to deal with pressure and constant physical activity. They learn patrolling, leadership, land navigation, and survival skills.

The second phase is mountain training. During Mountain Phase, soldiers learn how to climb down high cliffs at night with full packs. They also learn how to carry a wounded comrade. Swamp and jungle training is the third phase, called Florida Phase. Soldiers experience the kinds of extreme conditions they might have to deal with in combat. They take classes on avoiding poisonous snakes. They learn what to do if they are bitten. They learn the best ways to cross swamps and how to operate small boats. Finally, students load up rubber rafts called Zodiacs. They travel to an island in the Gulf of Mexico at night. They reach the shore and fight a simulated battle. They win by capturing the island.

Candidates must conquer all their fears to complete Ranger School.

TRAINING WITH LASERS

An important tool used in Ranger training is the Military Integrated Laser Engagement System, or MILES. One part of the MILES is a laser. It fits on the barrel of a rifle or machine gun. The weapon shoots blanks instead of bullets. The other part of the MILES is a sensor. The Rangers wear this on a harness. The Rangers use the MILES to practice fighting. If one Ranger shoots his opponent with his MILES laser, one sensor beeps to say the target was hit. It is like a military version of laser tag.

Ranger School candidates must pass a physical training test and a Ranger obstacle course. Trainees have to swim 50 feet (15 m) in their uniforms and boots. They must wear their equipment harnesses and carry their rifles. Then they remove their rifles and gear while underwater. One of the hardest tests is to walk off a 10-foot-high (3 m) diving platform while blindfolded. They must remove the blindfold and swim to the side of the pool without losing any equipment. They also cannot show fear or panic. But that's not all. The trainees must also be able to get down a cliff in bad weather. They march 8 miles (13 km) with 70-pound (32 kg) backpacks. There are classroom tests in map reading and writing battle plans too. If they fail, they can't sign up for Ranger School to try again. Only soldiers who drop out because of illness or injury can try again.

After they pass Ranger School, some graduates take a special training course in surveillance, tracking, and stalking. One test is finding a hidden stash of food with a map. If they don't find it, they don't eat.

Highly trained and highly effective, the 75th Ranger Regiment is the most elite infantry unit in the U.S. Army. The soldiers who wear the tan beret are always ready to lead the way.

GLOSSARY

ALLIED FORCES

friendly nations that often
help one another in wars; in
World War II, the twenty-
six countries, including the
United States, that fought
against the Axis powers
(Germany, Italy, Japan,
and others)

AMBUSH

surprise attack from a
hidden position

ASSAULT

military attack on enemy
forces

CAMOUFLAGE

disguising military
equipment or people by
covering or painting them
so that they blend in with
their surroundings

DEPLOY

to send a military unit on a
mission

FAST-ROPE

technique used to slide
down a rope from a
helicopter

MEDIC

a soldier who is specially
trained to give first aid in
combat

MORTAR

a weapon that fires
explosive shells upward
over buildings and hills

RECOIL

to spring back or rebound,
such as a gun after it fires

RECONNAISSANCE

secret information gathering

SURVEILLANCE

keeping a close watch on
something

TALIBAN

militant Islamic movement
of Pashtun tribesmen from
around Afghanistan

LEARN MORE

Further Reading

Adams, Simon. *Eyewitness Soldier*. New York: DK Publishing, 2009.

Alvarez, Carlos. *Army Rangers*. Minneapolis: Bellwether Media, 2010.

Cooke, Tim. *US Army Rangers*. New York: PowerKids Press, 2013.

Lusted, Marcia Amidon. *Army Delta Force: Elite Operations*. Minneapolis: Lerner Publications Company, 2014.

Websites

How Stuff Works: How the Army Rangers Work
http://science.howstuffworks.com/army-ranger3.htm
This website explains all about the Rangers, their history, their training, and their missions.

The 75th Ranger Regiment Official Website
http://www.goarmy.com/ranger.html
This website features information and videos about the 75th Ranger Regiment.

U.S. Army Rangers
http://www.army.mil/ranger/
The U.S. Army's website about the Rangers explains what the Rangers do and what training they must complete. It includes the Ranger Creed.

INDEX

About the Author

Marcia Amidon Lusted has written more than seventy-five books for young readers. She is also a magazine editor, a writing instructor, and a musician.